"*Frost & Pollen* is a verdant efflorescence or words blooming over an understory of myth, the lush foliage of its language, of desire and the garden, nature and humankind, balanced between Eros and Thanatos, between intimacy and danger, power and libido. It is a delight and a rich satisfaction to stray in the remarkable life and beauty of its lines. This is poetry filled with the force (and music) that drives the green fuse."

— GARY BARWIN, AUTHOR OF *FOR IT IS A PLEASURE AND
A SURPRISE TO BREATHE*

"Part eco-poetry, part Arthurian fan-fiction in verse, *Frost & Pollen* unfurls as a sustained meditation by a mature poet's hand. At once erotic—imagine Georgia O'Keeffe's floral paintings—and deliberately in dialogue with the earth, Hajnoczky presents a poetics that centres female pleasure and luxuriates in foliage, in imagery and language. Told partly from the perspective of the Green Knight, this work is mythical and imaginative, well-researched and deftly crafted. A delightful read."

— KLARA DU PLESSIS, AUTHOR OF *EKKE* AND
HELL LIGHT FLESH

"*Frost & Pollen* continues Helen Hajnoczky's spectacular inter-rogation of language and her experimentation with the porous boundaries between body and earth. Much like the language play of Gertrude Stein or Lisa Robertson, Hajnoczky's text gives language an intimate flavour but also transmutes the familiar into the foreign. Her open questioning brings in subjects as diverse as female desire, botany, and *Sir Gawain and the Green Knight*. Tense with desire, these powerful poems show once again that Hajnoczky's poetic eye is impeccable and her voice is one of the most assured in Canadian poetry."

— SANDY POOL, AUTHOR OF *EXPLODING INTO NIGHT* AND *UNDARK*

"Hajnoczky's language flowers with whorls of sonic splendour. In this embodied and ecological exploration, letters unfurl, and time collapses as medieval and millennial mysteries mingle in a forest of swerves that will leave readers enchanted. Touching her tongue to the roots of language, Hajnoczky deracinates exclusionary practices of listening, syntax, and meaning-making in a topology of rapture."

— SUZANNE ZELAZO, AUTHOR OF *LANCES ALL ALIKE* AND *PARLANCE*

FROST & POLLEN

Helen Hajnoczky

Invisible Publishing
Halifax & Prince Edward County

Library and Archives Canada Cataloguing in Publication

Title: Frost & pollen / Helen Hajnoczky.

Other titles: Frost and pollen

Names: Hajnoczky, Helen, author.

Description: Poems.

Identifiers: Canadiana 20210246367 | ISBN 9781988784809 (softcover)

Classification: LCC PS8615.A3857 F76 2021 | DDC C811/.6—dc23

Edited by Derek Beaulieu

Cover art: *Bouquet of Flowers in an Urn* (1724) by Jan van Huysum

Design by Megan Fildes

With thanks to type designer Rod McDonald

Invisible Publishing is committed to protecting our natural environment. As part of our efforts, both the cover and interior of this book are printed on acid-free 100% post-consumer recycled fibres.

Printed and bound in Canada

Invisible Publishing | Halifax & Prince Edward County

www.invisiblepublishing.com

We acknowledge for their financial support of our publishing program the Canada Council for the Arts, the Ontario Arts Council, and the Government of Canada.

 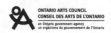 

"You gave me hyacinths first a year ago;
"They called me the hyacinth girl."

    — T. S. Eliot, *The Waste Land*

Mrs. Dalloway said she would buy the flowers herself.

    — Virginia Woolf, *Mrs Dalloway*

every horizon to a man. every solemn, always solemn. every sentence has a plan.

    — Natalie Simpson, *accrete or crumble*

BLOOM & MARTYR 1

FOLIAGE 65

BLOOM & MARTYR

If you were mine, lash and strawberry. If bound and frail, take charge of me. My caveat, your excavation. Tender crumpled, my blunder, your shoulder, my shorn or hollow. If you were mine, nectarine and cherish. If you were mine, what stings. Tell me brittle, slate and layered, touch me there.

Cinched and knotted, your welling, welling up. Stasis, I trace your spine. Tell me I am, tell me down or dappled and sugar swallow, tell me I am ripened, always ripening, tell me I am sweet.

Glisten, my plum, my causal, seared down to nausea, call me anything you like. Sundry, you lichen like a bit lip, lobed and salted, drawn and tactile, I could make you smile. Grown orchard, your rosehip, my petals, your knuckles forged or spring and frozen. I am melting, my sweet, your sweet thumbs, the frost is biting.

Come now, furled now, travel case and lily. Semi or my stomach bracket, snow and sprouting. If I forage, if I fold and pollen, if I should I should or fumble. Tell me if my lip, my crisp, my zipper silk or swollen, you swell like dust, like pollen. Touch me, my sign my omen, your bloom and nightshade, my lovely rhododendron, my lovely silk and rotten.

Your blush, my chrysanthemum. Your winter frost, dahlia and molten. My shoulder blades, raspberry and tarnish. Your breath, bloom and hemlock. Your frost, your flush, cold blossom, my mouth.

Tell me fortunate and columbine, I broke your coarse
or sullen. My venation, I venerate you, my whorl, my
entire margin. Filigree and spring, my lilac, my not yet,
you could lie back. Your rough or tulip, bed still frozen.
Choose my dear, choose and vestige, spreading open.

Ebb this even. Caved in, I am cooled, I am copper. Scoured like water, like nectar. Tell me your smooth and forward. Tell me grace or portal. Tell me, tell me my tumbling and orbital. Corrosive, this caustic nonsense, this shadow or shade. You place your slender fingers, your wake. My carnage, my calamity, please shade me.

Bent daisy, bent or better. You are my letter, my salient, my ladle of censure. My taste this corded or cradled. You are my sudden, your foresight, your rib cage, my taste buds. Flowered, forgive me please forgive me again.

Stolen or spoil, come glass or iron, teach me, my rose, my rise, your hollow. I will follow. My columbine, my clatter, your abdomen, your wade or tidal. Spring rain, tell me agate, tell me granular, tell me again, my candid, your molar, your morbid or shroud. Tell me my waist or gentle. Pull back and gentle, so gentle. Let me follow.

Hardly your hail bent bluster or summer. My beaded now blister, shame or summer. Your harvest, this pummel, this basket, this shovel. Pluck or shaken, ready, I am reasonable. I am not at all reasonable. My warm muzzle, my maiden, my gravel. Your palm, your funnel. Callous or carried, come now. I am a column, I will grovel. My hyacinth, I will grovel.

Corrugate or crave, my stomach ache, my sorrow. Your forage or stable, your tangle, your tingle. Make me sudden, make me stable. Please make me please. Your thrust, my martyr, my marrow.

Mesh and modelled, pharmacological. You are mottled, my molten, my gored or spoken. Your whisper, your slip, my slip, a torn violet, I am waiting. Make me trodden or saline, make me ragged. Deep violet, a violet is deep and bruised.

Place splayed or sharpen, my failing, your pollen. Blossom forged or autumn. My failing, I am fallen. You light or soften, your tryst or season. Cave me in my red nettle, my stinging thistle. My bite or arrow, my poison, your strap, your cinch, your harrow. My violet, make me grovel.

Your grip, my wrists. Floral or sundial. Show me sly now, show me grave or atom. Slid your stride, your organic and cavern. Show me how to nascent, blatant or eroded. Show me my stagger, my shattered and stolen gaze. Show me how to be your lantern, your lily. Show me corrupted, your flay, your floral. Leave me molten, mottled, leave me open and swallow.

Sugar crystal or frostbite, tell me trill and amethyst, tell me anything you like. My pastel, my posies, my morrow, my bare soil. Please tell me, tell me planned or torrid. Tell me my order, my slender, your forefinger, you stretch along me, your weight, make me wait. Darling, please break me frost or fever scrape me, and secret, please break me further. Your frill, your breath, your frost, you break me.

Your thirst, your forearm. Tell me dry and haven, tell me tight and bloom. Crocus and forbade, your ash and graven. My crave, my cranberry, your switch, cacti or avid. You hover, your blossom, your desert, my desert, your crystal and shattered. You crush me, please crush me, and crush me again. The sand.

Your index, you unfurl me. My caution, your caustic, unfurl me. Your caress or crux, your planted your must. I will for you slowly, as you instruct. Instruct me, I must.

Startled gash or lashes, your trembling, my ossuary.
Your filaments, my quick or glowing. Slow now lament,
I filigree your mourning. Moss or lichen, bound though
low, my coral your core, your chorus my void. Try or
field, your pen my hand, your pain my plan. Make me
lament, your lashes glowing, make me glint.

Peony and repent, a peony is penance. Teased and finite, fodder with all your might. Glare, your ankles, your knees, your hips and daring. Darned or forgotten, stitch, my buds, my blossom, the same now. Make me perennial. Make me your thorn and hook now, heavy flower. Make me keep seasons, make me flower.

My territory, your glow. My path, your footprints pocket sore, your sore, your firm and waiting. Hold my torn, my strewn, my pale or petal. Dazed or garden, sore gardenia. Pummel hail and focus. Make me still or strewn, your shorn boast and territory. Pin me, moth or flower, settle in and tear me. Your stamen your mouth, your scandal, please tear me.

Cairn, sweet cairn, my border guard. Your flower bed, my corroded sense, your pose and portion fairly. Your shiver, your meld, your seedling. Your position, your gravity. Stern, carry on, you pose me. You seed me, parch me, sway me. Stern, your guarded portion firm, you parch me.

Chokecherry your palm, threaded or drain. Bitter, your letting, you let me swelter. Choke or stasis, your rigid or botanic. You make me stiff and verdant, you make me harden, cherry, choke or poison, you make me open.

Grace, you raze me, moth and flutter. Temperate and dahlia, my joints, your pressure. Roots or twine, you entwine me. Hewn now, rotten moult, you melt me. Bind and gag me, sweet sour cherry.

Beguile my guilt, your force slip and muddy. Your fertile and nectar, this glimmer and plant me. Photosynthetic and sensitive, my darling, synthesize me. Chlorophyll and sugar, your crucible, so luminous, crystallize me.

Your vexed and tendril, columbine, each petal forged and broken. My borrowed, my rhododendron, my honeyed amber, my raw clay, my sordid violet spoken. Blazon, my sweet, my hurricane. Your vines, each tendril, each tender, and forge me. You vex me. My twirl and flame, my columbine, my honeyed storm, you vex me.

Henbane, my saccharine sting. Scraped or borrowed, your neck, your chest, my fallen and floral. Fallen dew, my wretched hollow collarbone. Toxic and morose, your throat, my swallow. Wallow in me, my potent spoil. You hollow me.

Sugar plum, cider sunk or bitten. My portent, your votive, this leaf, this fern, your careful candour. Your languor, your empire. Flayed or unfolding, stranded and bite me. My sanguine earnest, a bundle of fern, sweet frost or regal. My scrub, my gushing willow, my wound, make me swallow.

My orchid, my torment, tell me how or fragrant. Slag or slacken, your rigid blue or torrid. Quarry, dry roots, your torrent sleet and sudden. Hold me, hold me still. Metamorphic, your magma, my marigold and still. My floral torrent, you sear me.

Anguish and binding, a begonia is contrite. Shy, the garden bedding. Shrug, my cleft, my porous notion. Your shoulders or quarrel, my quaint rosewater, your strict embers, you grow me. Engulf or stipple, ablaze, your strict, your own, you scald me.

You make me ritual and incensed. Mist or mortal, your conclusion, my cordoned soul. Blessed, my orchid, my futile. Vain and fodder, your vein, my florid struggle. You make me steady, my petal, my pewter, my kneeling, make me kneel. Your grip, you make me ache or kneeling furrow, make me bow.

My fever, my poinsettia, your traction or tryst. Subside and swoon, my frost, your breath. Frayed and gloaming, your property or whim. My corset, my feeble battle, your blush, my tactic, coronate and spindle. You twist me. Feverish and unravel me. My point, my fever, my poinsettia, you fray me.

My mouth, your fodder. Your mouth, my magnolia.
Sugar cane me, your eloquence and softer. My sweet,
all told, you tell me. My breath, you breathe. Wilt, you
wilt me. You make it hard to breathe.

Darned or moral, your formal setting. Tell me through your crisp and spoil. My fond and common, your starch and oral. My dahlia, your nectar, impressed or stolen. Your imprint, your foil. Your scar and crystalline, please press me down. My dahlia, my fissure, your crown.

Ginger and sing, I'm ailing. Your measure of strict and yet. You won't let or parse me, this flood or tiding. Let me run my stasis, your clavicle or sudden. You leave me ailing, moment hung. Your letting, my static, your sting, your thumb. Have my cavern, my mordant, your thrum.

Grim and fragrant, daft foil, I preen in your shards. In vain or staccato, my reflection, your rooted and gossamer. Tell me how your stiff, your ardour, arm my pallor. My daffodil, your pristine splinter. My foliage and dwindle, your switch and stiff, you sharpen me. Foiled and glimmer, please shatter me.

Vertebrae and acute. Snapped ragged supplicant. Your firm pouring or drought. My fragments or tainted. Tell me to take this, fragrant or sacred. My careful your cannon, my strain and vivid. Your axiom, humble or caramel, make me your floret, your noun. My lovely snapdragon, spinal and splendid, make me your noun.

Your inflorescence, my indolence or stigma. My corolla, your whorl or forgone. Your anther, my tongue. Make me flourish and florid, spread my sepals, your petiole, my calyx, tell me to bud. Your anther, my undoing. Your anther, my tongue.

Petals numb, you mute my swollen blossoms. Buds all thumbs, your bloom, my chrysanthemum. My headlong or heavenly, your cleft and sweet. Floral blotch, too thick, too heavy to speak. Make me your abundant or dour, your abandon, make me bow. My sweet, my swollen blossom. Make me bow.

Plum blush all show, you could eat me whole. My shawls or petals, your veils enrobed. Violet and sugar, my crystalline, your snow. Huddle or soil, your sordid glow. Make me furl or shadow stringent, you could eat me whole.

Grapple dormant, your gradient, fold and dry me. My cloy, your sentry. My mellow, your treaty. Hinder or torrent, my pliable, your mastery. Your mimic, my sample, drastic and pin me. My flagrant, lance and border, please ply me.

Your hex, my failing, a blueberry is blue and shameful. My dandelion, your escape and salient, my lips and penchant, your palm or pendant. Tell me valley, tell me sorrow grave and statement. Call me to you, I will come.

Delirium, your masterpiece, my minimum and process. My protest, your pendulum, my lovely phosphorescence. My lick, my fathom. Laudanum and springtime, make me dictate, your neck, my crest, your wake. Your torrent and trailing, please wake me.

First chill then stupor, excess and ardour. My rose, your rise, you flatter me. Hollyhock and shatter me. Your vestige, my deference, flatter me. Sweet ventricle, sweet peony.

Pantomime or prim. My pith, your feast. Clatter, your dulcet feats, you feast in me. Nevertheless, my foreshadowing. Sod or sediment, your forbidden laurel, substantiate me. Clementine and denigrate me. Your thorns and laurel salivate, your foreshadowing, please forbid me.

Phalaenopsis, you wipe my mouth off with your thumb. Your stature, white petals, white-blue sepals. My columbine, your drove, orchid and contaminant. My mouth and supple dormant, wipe my mouth off with your rose.

Hydrangea, I oblige. Your gossamer and choler, your choler and deprived. Concave my floret budding, your blazon and sordid rosy. Try me, I try to sweetly. My sweet choler, close your eyes.

My darling, my dire. Crepe paper and crumpled alter. A stocking is silk and folded blind. Your rose, my rosehip, take your time. Whorl enough, my wrought iron, winding and tipple, you take your time.

Your current, my poppy. Salt or seed me. Your stamen, blot me. Tell me what would make you happy. Stretch my temperate, my drenched or fortune. Pit and quandary, tell me how to bend. So a thimble is heavy, efflorescent and contrite.

Your stumble, my sanctum, you make me thorough.
Drag me through to tremble. Make me your wreath,
your narrow. My gamble, your lush and spurn. Bulb or
furtive pebble, force my stumble. Your ripple, my blush
unravels.

Each budding thorn, each sprouting thistle. My stalwart, your predicate, my attrition, my thermion, my truss. Dormant, the lattice foiled when the snow comes. Gnarled iron, the winter garden rosy cold, the winter garden flush.

Hibernate and trill, my flourish, my hydrangea. Stranded, my freesia, your torpor, your brim, collateral and tremble. Your roots, your soil, extended and meander. Your interspersed and your treason, my lovely, my hydrangea.

Permeate and dazed, my daisies frost and wilt. I will, I will my arch and cornice. A garden sleeps or hardened shudder, your dawn or torment, cantankerous or sore. But in relief my fierce and convalescent, your slumber ore. Awry, please permeate me. My frost, my wilted daisy.

Our terrarium, our lethargy. My darling, moths have no mouths. We gorge, so relentless, our opulent nests. We are restless, we are hungry. Butterfly, my shrug, your cocoon your flutter. My lepidoptera, my mouth, exuberant and hunger, kiss me. My darling, my flutter, your regal, opulent mouth, kiss me again.

Quartz and taciturn, your shock and forbidden zeal. My debris, earth and barter, your smile, blatant and budding. Corporeal, undermined, my skin. If shards or flagrant, my soporific, your grin. The snow accentuated and drifts, and so we drift. Let it sink in.

Vagrant, my nightshade or weeds. Your breath, your zephyr, fortified and stumbling, your gaze. Drastic, your slender dram. My hands and roses, your roses crisp and capable. Your hands warm and spring, sweet seedling. My courtesan, my chamomile. My fortunate, my nightly dreams. My sweet, my stumble, sweet seedling.

Your tempered phrase, annotate and fuchsia. The tipple of buds, the mud, my seraphim and rising. Nod or blazon, neither me, nor you, but a bluebell, courteous and cloister. Hibernate and fuchsia, a bluebell is stripped, and rising stippled, trills.

My freesia, your fumble frozen. Frost and fallen, the sleet, my dear, is building. Neither dour nor amnesty and spoken, my one, my only. Frail, the stalk is broken. My thaw and bitter formulate, this flourish I'm forgotten. My sweet, my frost, my coronate. My dear, the stalk is broken.

Laced geranium, the catastrophic gloom. My fable ordained, crimson, your wade and angle, my draped, my drowsed, my armature and foil. Honeysuckle, berate, your lattice, no matter, little flower. You are my catastrophe.

Distraught, a daisy wavered and able. You thumb each petal. My oblige and plotted, your fervour like ice, like velvet. A breath and frost is velvet. Sugar entwined and speckle, a daisy scattered like ice, like petals. Brilliant and snow, the daisies.

Chamomile and anguish, sweet hyacinth. My rotten, my cordial. Your antidote, orb of wrist bone and careful, my arms full of chamomile. A hyacinth and cordial, you sweeten me.

My bloom and martyr, your marrow, my morrow. A hyacinth forgives, your frost and haven, your lily and forgotten. We bloom and hibernate, filament or fragrant. Your lavender, my languid or begotten. Beguiled each, we blossom.

FOLIAGE

PASSUS I

When Hades had his fill of hurling flames and catapulting comets
The churning magma mellowed, smothering Earth's embers,
Then in the Archean the Earth's crust cooled into continents,
And the original organisms stirred in the oceans exhaling oxygen,
Then in the Paleozoic primordial plants populated Pangaea,
Ordovician swamps were festooned with the spores of tiny shoots,
And in the Devonian, carbon dioxide doused Earth's dewy gardens,
And, at last, Archaeopteris ascended into the ancient atmosphere,
Wrenching its wooden roots into the sod and clod and clay,
Breaking rocks and stones to nourish ponds and waterways.
                    So trees
            Shaped this world
            With green and ease,
            While regal ferns unfurled
            In splendid filigrees.

Then when the World wanted ornament, Flora in her flowing robes
Gifted flowers to the leas that flourished and fragranced the winds.
With her every step, sweet spices sprang forth to flavour the fields,
And then, before her dance was done, she knelt down to the ground
And placing her palm on the merry moss moving to her music
She conjured me to keep watch over the trees and ferns and flowers,
The holy holly and blooming baubles that adorn her dominion,
The roots and rot that sprout and feed the fauna that walk the Earth.
And so the boughs burgeoned and blossomed, flourished and failed,
And I dozed—drowsed by the harmonies of life's rhythms.

    These isles
   Were then disturbed by the arrival of men,
   Desecrating the forest with destruction so vile,
   Until I awoke to restore tranquility when
   The woods called on me for my axe and for my guile.

Stirred from my slumber in the sumptuous moss, moist with snow,
I awakened at Yuletide, when the evergreens grow flush with frost
And the ivy glistens in glittering garlands of cold crystals.
My juniper beard studded with snowflakes and lichens,
I wrested the roots of my arms from the dirt, my legs from the land,
And standing full and viridescent, I straightened and stretched.
And there, buried beside my bed, in a blanket of botanical debris
Was my axe, still grand and massive but dulled by dulcet peace.
Kneeling, I prised the prize from the placid patch of plants
And heaved this heavy honour high above my head.
                    And so
          To play fate's game
          In my heart I know
          I must seek Morgan le Fay, the dame
          Who can sharpen this blade of woe.

Wandering the woods I wend my way to the water
And behold at the place where the boughs bend open
A glade, glistening with a lagoon ringed by a granite beach,
And there, in the tempest, a sorceress stands in a clearing of calm
Where no wind can disturb her, no cold can cool her,
And the ferns and flowers and fronds thrive in her Spring.
My soul so satisfied by the sight of this enchantress,
I lay my axe my troth my heart my life at her charmed feet,
And this bewitching beauty bends to take my hand and the handle,
And leading me to the lagoon she draws the axe across a stone.

        My blade
    Now sharp and true,
    I embrace my mate, my maid,
    She whispers her wit so shrewd
    Of how we should stage our charade.

I am the bite, the bitter brethren of the branches left to men's mercy.
Tied to the Earth, they cannot fight the foul forest-mangling mortals
Who wreck the woodlands and demolish the meadows,
Those vile villains who vex the venerable Earth that privileged them,
That gave them shade and shelter and sustenance and pleasure,
Men, who felled the forest to fuel their fires and fashion their turrets.
And so my quest is to quell the cupidity of these cavaliers—
To sow a seed of foreboding in their stomachs at their holiday feast.
My gift will grow into a notion that will gnaw at their feeble wits—
That if they abuse the abundance of Eden, the garden will strike back
                    through me—
          I am the defender
          Of the woods and trees,
          And men's tormenter
          With tricks and mysteries.

On my crusade to the castle I collect my exuberance and buoyancy.
I bow to each copse, my eyes crisp and crimson like holly berries.
My kin, my kind, the twinkling of thickets and thorns sparks in me
Notions for the particulars of the Christmas contest to challenge the
Cavalrymen of Camelot, who cut the flora down for their comfort—
They chop and scorch and squander the bounty of the Earth,
Confident the uncultivated acres will come blooming back—
So the game on which they will gamble their gallantry and goodness
Will be twisted like a vine twining up the towers of their towns.
And as I decide the details of how to deceive the dubious champions
    I arrive
   At the chateaux,
   And to its gates I ride—
   To see what I might bestow,
   To see what I might contrive.

Battering their barricades and bursting their doors
I bash booming into their boisterous banquet,
The silly aristocrats suddenly silent but for gasps,
I shift my axe from hand to hand, so the blade and hilt
Glint in the glimmering glow of their gilded gala.
All are breathless at my burly oaken brawn.
Then, bellowing in my best beastly bark,
With withering weightiness I wail *Wher is*
Þe gouernour of þis gyng? Gladly I wolde
Se þat segg in syȝt, and with hymself speke
raysoun.
    The knights cower
    And the ladies swoon.
    To my terrifying power
    No mortal is immune.

Their mortifyingly meager monarch, in man's manner,
Entreats me to engage in their eating and enjoy their ease—
In this hall, where the holly they hacked from its home hangs,
This room, where the wood they wounded burns to coal—
The idea that I would enjoy this insulting auditorium
Makes me emerald with enflamed temper.
These measly men whose mansion is ornamented
With wilting boughs and imitation wrought-iron wood,
Whose windows are wound with drawings of flowers,
Deign to think I'd dine at their dead table.
                    This feast
            Will soon come to an end,
            Not in a sigh of peace,
            But with one condemned
            When my contest has ceased.

The moment for my and Morgan's game nigh, I say

Nay, as help me, he þat on hyȝe syttes,
To wone any quyle in þis won, hit watz not myn ernde;
Bot for þe los of þe, lede, is lyft vp so hyȝe,
And þy burȝ and þy burnes best ar holden,
Stifest vnder stel-gere on stedes to ryde,
Þe wyȝtest and þe worþyest of þe worldes kynde,
Preue for to play wyth in oþer pure laykez,
And here is kydde cortaysye, as I haf herd carp,
And þat hatz wayned me hider, iwyis, at þis tyme.
Ȝe may be seker bi þis braunch þat I bere here
Þat I passe as in pes, and no plyȝt seche;
For had I founded in fere in feȝtyng wyse,
I haue a hauberghe at home and a helme boþe,
A schelde and a scharp spere, schinande bryȝt,
Ande oþer weppenes to welde, I wene wel, als;
Bot for I wolde no were, my wedez ar softer.
Bot if þou be so bold as alle burnez tellen,
Þou wyl grant me godly þe gomen þat I ask
                    bi ryȝt.

> And their credulous king swears
> Whatever game might be my wish
> A knight there will accept my dare—
> A fool whose honour I will squish.

Guaranteed an engagement I lay down the gauntlet—
Nay, frayst I no fy3t, in fayth I þe telle,
Hit arn aboute on þis bench bot berdlez chylder.
If I were hasped in armes on a he3e stede,
Here is no mon me to mach, for my3tez so wayke.
Forþy I craue in þis court a Crystemas gomen,
For hit is 3ol and Nwe 3er, and here ar 3ep mony:
If any so hardy in þis hous holdez hymseluen,
Be so bolde in his blod, brayn in hys hede,
Þat dar stifly strike a strok for an oþer,
I schal gif hym of my gyft þys giserne ryche,
Þis ax, þat is heué innogh, to hondele as hym lykes,
And I schal bide þe fyrst bur as bare as I sitte.
If any freke be so felle to fonde þat I telle,
Lepe ly3tly me to, and lach þis weppen,
I quit-clayme hit for euer, kepe hit as his auen,
And I schal stonde hym a strok, stif on þis flet,
Ellez þou wyl di3t me þe dom to dele hym an oþer
                    barlay,
            And 3et gif hym respite,
            A twelmonyth and a day;
            Now hy3e, and let se tite
            Dar any herinne o3t say.

I cast the crimson crystals of my eyes around the castle—
None of these knights have the nerve to take up my challenge.
My trick has tickled me, and trashed their troth in timidity.
To spite these spineless soldiers I ask *What, is þis Arthures hous,*
Þat al þe rous rennes of þurȝ ryalmes so mony?
Where is now your sourquydrye and your conquestes,
Your gryndellayk and your greme, and your grete wordes?
Now is þe reuel and þe renoun of þe Rounde Table
Ouerwalt wyth a worde of on wyȝes speche,
For al dares for drede withoute dynt schewed!

Shamefaced,

They sit in silence,
Their court disgraced
By the threat of violence,
Their holiday mirth debased.

And Arthur, annoyed by his faint-hearted allies,
To halt the humiliation says he'll hack off my head—
Then, at last, a lad lets his morals clobber his fearfulness.
As Morgan anticipated, Sir Gawain approaches and asserts
To Arthur and to all the aristocrats that he will heave my axe. I ask
Refourme we oure forwardes, er we fyrre passe.
Fyrst I eþe þe, haþel, how þat þou hattes
Þat þou me telle truly, as I tryst may.
In courtly form, the soldier identifies himself as Gawain,
And the lad agrees, giving his guarantee, approving our pact.

> I heave
> The rules out like a thorny vine
> *Sir Gawan, so mot I þryue*
> *As I am ferly fayn*
> *Þis dint þat þou schal dryue.*

Bigog, Sir Gawan, me lykes
Þat I schal fange at þy fust þat I haf frayst here.
And þou hatz redily rehersed, bi resoun ful trwe,
Clanly al þe couenaunt þat I þe kynge asked,
Saf þat þou schal siker me, segge, bi þi trawþe,
Þat þou schal seche me þiself, where-so þou hopes
I may be funde vpon folde, and foch þe such wages
As þou deles me to-day bifore þis douþe ryche.
Before his brethren the boy must bow—
For he has held up his own hand

> to bear
>> My scorn for man's evils—
>> We'll see how he fairs
>> Burdened with this primeval
>> Bondage he now wears.

His eyes betray his terror of entering the unknown—
Of the occult mastery of the ancient trees and thickets.
He pleads to know the place of my chapel, and I say
Þat is innogh in Nwe Ʒer, hit nedes no more.
Ʒif I þe telle trwly, quen I þe tape haue
And þou me smoþely hatz smyten, smartly I þe teche
Of my hous and my home and myn owen nome,
Þen may þou frayst my fare and forwardez holde;
And if I spende no speche, þenne spedez þou þe better,
For þou may leng in þy londe and layt no fyrre—
                    bot slokes!
          Ta now þy grymme tole to þe,
          And let se how þou cnokez.
          Gawain agrees and picks up the blade—
          My enchanted axe holding his focus.

So the snare is set and I will soon sow the lesson
That hacking and harvesting the heart of the wild
Is tempting a tempest that no mortal can manage—
That man's abominable acts against his habitat
Come with a consequence that he must contend with.
I kneel and carefully comb my crown of verdant curls
To expose my naked neck for the knight to carve.
A prisoner of our pact the paladin picks up the axe—
Heaves it so hard it hacks into the ground, but to his horror
Without wincing I wait for my head to halt its rolling.
                    I glare
            At Gawain from my severed head,
            And pick my crown up by the hair,
            Watching his eyes blossom with dread
            As I grin with wild delight and declare—

Loke, Gawan, þou be grayþe to go as þou hettez,
And layte as lelly til þou me, lude, fynde,
As þou hatz hette in þis halle, herande þise knyȝtes;
To þe grene chapel þou chose, I charge þe, to fotte
Such a dunt as þou hatz dalt—disserued þou habbez
To be ȝederly ȝolden on Nw ȝeres morn.
Þe knyȝt of þe grene chapel men knowen me mony;
Forþi me for to fynde if þou fraystez, faylez þou neuer.
Þerfore com, oþer recreaunt be calde þe behoues.
My dangling head delivering this devastating dare,
                    I mount
            My mighty steed of moss and leaves
            To ride swiftly back to the glen to recount
            To Morgan the tale of the knight now aggrieved
            Left with a long year of dreadful days to count.

I gallop to the glen where my gracious Fay awaits,
And she lovingly lays her mystical hands upon my laceration,
And twigs begin to twine there where blood had rushed.
Healed and whole and happy, I hoist her heavenwards and
Lay her in the lush lea, where she plants her gentle lips upon me.
Drawing with her forefinger a five-pointed pentacle, first upon
My breast, and then again on her belly, we embrace,
Entwined in the twisting gossamer grasses of our glade.
We doze until dawn's dew settles in our drowsy mead,
And wake in the wonder that once our hoax is concluded
                  our child
           Will be born to bear the grudge
           Of any wild land these men defile—
           She will serve as nature's judge,
           Upon whom the goddess Flora will smile.

My formidable sorceress then commences conjuring—
Drawing with a jade dagger in the dirt our five-pointed pentacle,
And petitioning the planet's potency, she pulls up from the plain
A captivating chapel of creeping vines and cascading orchids—
From here my power pulses like Spring pumping in my veins.
Next, my enchantresses entreats a nearby glen to give her grace
To raise the ramparts of a radiant fortress from the dirt, and for
The birds and beasts to appear as people—ladies and knights—
Until Gawain comes to contravene our covenant in his cowardice.
Last, my lady transfigures me to a man and her form to a matron and
               we wait
          Until the unworthy knight has arrived
          To open the star-crossed gate—
          To step into the snare we have contrived.
          He approaches—our prey tempted by our bait.

PASSUS II

We wait while Winter wears away and Spring sprouts its sprigs.
We wait while the Summer sun shines, then succumbs to Autumn.
We wait while Fall's fanciful leaves fail and fade. We wait until
Yule yet again lays its veil of snow upon the evergreens.
While waiting my wife and her forest-folk feast on flowers and
Dance to the meadow's delicate melodies, the birds and breeze,
Perfecting their appearance as princes and princesses for Gawain.
All the while I wait in my chapel, channeling the ancient magic
Of field and forest, ferns and florets, up through my feet—
The might of the meadow thumping through my veins

                    until

        Morgan rouses me from my rumination
        To bring to fruit the forest's will.
        I offer the woods my final words of oblation,
        And my prayer said, we prepare for the thrill.

My lady leads me to the lake, and leaning into the waves, she lifts out
A new Norse axe, sharp and shiny—a wild weapon of the woods—
And we leave this cleaver on the chapel altar for later in our plot.
Our jaunty troupe departs, travelling contentedly to our fortress folly.
Casting charms, my enchantress decorates the citadel for Christmas.
Last, she spells a sparrow into the semblance of a spouse for me—
A temptress to trick the banneret who will traipse into our castle.
As my Fairy informed us he would, Gawain arrives at our banquet,
And I say *ʒe ar welcum to welde as yow lykez*
Þat here is; al is yowre awen, to haue at yowre wylle
                    and welde.

                The gullible Gawain is so grateful for our hearth
                That he has no suspicion our mansion is spelled,
                Or that soon the sparrow damsel will ensnare his heart.
                This Yuletide it will be not the trees but he who is felled.

The next night I begin to ensnare the knight in our net,
Issuing an invitation that will embed itself in his mind.
I say *And I schal fonde, bi my fayth, to fylter wyth þe best*
Er me wont þe wede, with help of my frendez.
No Arthurian man-at-arms can abstain from accepting a challenge
Nor can such a knight ignore a noble's compliment.
To ensure the snare is snug on the soldier's soul I say
Iwysse sir, quyl I leue, me worþez þe better
Þat Gawayn hatz ben my gest at Goddez awen fest.
After a year of dreading this adventure and his debt,
                    the knight
            Here in our manor feels so secure,
            That his fear of his fate in his upcoming fight
            Will lead him to happily leap into our lure,
            Where he'll be forced to face my new axe's might.

In the depths of this enchanted manor I ask the knave to stay,
To celebrate Christmas in our cheery castle, and he breaks—
Admitting he is aimlessly ambling these lands, lost and lonely,
And when Gawain whines that he cannot complete his quest without
At last locating the emerald chapel, I laugh *Now leng þe byhoues,*
For I schal teche yow to þat terme bi þe tymez ende,
Þe grene chapayle vpon grounde greue yow no more;
Bot ȝe schal be in yowre bed, burne, at þyn ese,
Quyle forth dayez, and ferk on þe fyrst of þe ȝere,
And cum to þat merk at mydmorn, to make quat yow likez
                    in spenne.
              Dowellez whyle New ȝeres daye,
              And rys, and raykez þenne,
              Mon schal yow sette in waye,
              Hit is not two myle henne.

Not sensing my subterfuge, the grateful Gawain agrees to stay,
So I ask 3e han demed to do þe dede þat I bidde;
Wyl 3e halde þis hes here at þys onez? and he agrees again.
For 3e haf trauayled, I say, laying my trap towen fro ferre,
And syþen waked me wyth, 3e arn not wel waryst
Nauþer of sostnaunce ne of slepe, soþly I knowe;
3e schal lenge in your lofte, and ly3e in your ese
To-morn quyle þe messequyle, and to mete wende
When 3e wyl, wyth my wyf, þat wyth yow schal sitte
And comfort yow with compayny, til I to cort torne;
                  3e lende,
       And I schal erly ryse,
       On huntyng wyl I wende.
       Considering this a deal to seize—
       Considering me his devoted friend.

I feel the forest's force flowing through my form—
Now I will nail down this knight like his kin would a board.
Ʒet firre, I say, laying my last trap, *a forwarde we make:*
Quat-so-euer I wynne in þe wod hit worþez to yourez,
And quat chek so ʒe acheue chaunge me þerforne.
Swete, swap we so, sware with trawþe,
Queþer, leude, so lymp, lere oþer better.
Not knowing the nefarious nature of this gamble
Gawain again acquiesces to my wager, so I ask
Who bryngez vus þis beuerage, þis bargayn is maked and
                    we toast
            To the seasonal days of feasting and fun—
            Him thinking me a gracious host,
            And yet, when our deal is done,
            He'll regret his pact with this forest ghost.

With Gawain off to bed to dream of and dread the day he will
Enter the enchanted evergreen glade around my chapel—
While he worries and wonders what awful woe awaits him—
Morgan and I make merry, our magic to manifest in mere days.
At midnight we meander to the meadow by the mansion,
And Morgan transforms a garland of ivy into a graceful garter
Of glimmering gossamer gold and glistening green glossy silk,
Which soon our sweet sparrow-damsel will use
To tempt the gent who now twists and turns in his bed.
And at last Morgan takes a sprig of holly
               so bright,
        With three shining berries,
        To resurrect a beast each night,
        With incantations of the Fairies,
        To seal the fate of our visiting knight.

PASSUS III

My men and I head to the hills to hunt the hart,
And seizing the stag I hand-feed the creature
One holly berry bewitched by my wife, so the
Death I deal will be but a brief semblance.
Meanwhile, our sparrow sings to Gawain her song
To trick and tempt him to trust in her trill.
As I kill the deer, she kisses the knight carefully.
Later that night, in the manor, I give Gawain his gift
And ask *How payez yow þis play? Haf I prys wonnen?*
Haue I þryuandely þonk þurȝ my craft serued?

                Gawain
        Calls this death—
        This display of pain—
        This creature robbed of breath—
        The most majestic he's seen slain.

Playing the part I pronounce *And al I gif ẏow, Gawayn,*
For by acorde of couenaunt ȝe craue hit as your awen.
The horseman then hands over his half of the pact,
Coming close to kiss me on my concealed green neck
Hit is god, I state in my stately way, *grant mercy þerfore.*
Hit may be such hit is þe better, and ȝe me breue wolde
Where ȝe wan þis ilk wele bi wytte of yorseluen.
The silly soul says his morals won't let him say.
I propose we play our parts again the next day and
Agreeing, the knight makes his way to nod and nap.

                    My wife
            Then takes me and the hart outside,
            Where she calls it back to life
            Using the spelled holly leaf, as if flesh lied—
            Her magic undoing all death's strife.

And once our brother the hart has happily hopped off,
I draw on Morgan's abdomen the five-pointed pentacle
That sustains our spell, and I plant the peck I procured
On her stomach, which swells to one third the size of
Our child, who will be born to fulfill the forest's wrath and fury.
In the morning I make my way again to the misty mounts where
I kill a boar, to whom I feed a berry, making death but temporary,
Whilst our sparrow kisses our knight twice. At our dinner I say
Now, Gawayn, presenting the boar's corpse, *þis gomen is your awen
Bi fyn forwarde and faste, faythely ʒe knowe.* He accepts it, and
        the beau
    Kisses me twice. I say, *Bi saynt Gile,*
    ʒe ar þe best þat I knowe!
    ʒe ben ryche in a whyle,
    Such chaffer and ʒe drowe.

Our trade completed, I try to tempt the tense knight
To stay and try our entertainment a third time,
But the bumbling brute is bothered by his bond—
By visions of vines vivisecting his veins,
By night terrors of trees cutting his tendons,
By dread-filled dreams of me dealing him his death—
Though he knows not that I am in fact his adversary.
Feeling the forest flourish in my soul, with potent charm
I convince the aristocrat he cannot vacate the castle
And that a good guest would give our game one last go
                        for joy
            And for good cheer of the season.
            He does not know he is our toy,
            He does not know my treason—
            Or that his troth I will destroy.

I tell him *As I am trwe segge, I siker my trawþe*
Þou schal cheue to þe grene chapel þy charres to make,
Leude, on Nw 3erez ly3t, longe bifore pryme.
Forþy þow lye in þy loft and lach þyn ese,
And I schal hunt in þis holt, and halde þe towchez,
Chaunge wyth þe cheuisaunce, bi þat I charre hider;
For I haf fraysted þe twys, and faythful I fynde þe.
Now "þrid tyme þrowe best" þenk on þe morne,
Make we mery quyl we may and mynne vpon joye,
For þe lur may mon lach when-so mon lykez.

                    He'll stay,
            He says, relieved and persuaded
            That there's no harm in one more day.
            Not knowing he could have evaded
            The shameful price he'll have to pay.

And again as the moon rises over the forest
Morgan restores the boar and I bend to her belly
To draw the star and impart the pair of kisses I won.
And again, her abdomen swells, now to two-thirds
The size of our child, who will revile the violence of man,
And defend the woodlands from his destruction.
That night Morgan made her way to the sparrow-maid's
Room, and according to our ruse, presented her
With the green and gold garter that will guarantee
That Gawain's weakness will reveal itself—his

               Terror
        Of meeting me at my chapel
        Will lead to the shameful error
        With which he will fail to grapple—
        His desire to be the garter's wearer.

At first light I ride with my knights to the ridge and intercept
A fox to whom I feed one red, Fairy-charmed fruit
Rendering the calamity of its slaughter temporary.
After attacking the animal I aim my course home, to return
To the manor where this ruse will reach its resolution.
When I enter the enchanted castle the cavalryman caller
Strides to my side to present me with three kisses.
Bi Kryst, I try to tickle his guilt, *ʒe cach much sele*
In cheuisaunce of þis chaffer, ʒif ʒe hade goud chepez.
He pleads that the price isn't the point if he paid
                    his debt,
            But I know the dishonest deception
            That is making him squirm and sweat,
            Hoping tomorrow for a safer reception
            When he faces my formidable threat.

Concealed in his cupboard is the cincture he covets—
The girdle that does not guard against green ghouls,
But that will destine this dolt to dishonour and disrepute—
His dimwittedness dooms him to disgrace in the woodland.
Keeping my promise to this duplicitous puerile paladin,
Mary, I exclaim, emphasizing my integrity, *myn is bihynde,*
For I haf hunted al þis day, and noȝt haf I geten
Bot þis foule fox felle—þe fende haf þe godez!—
And þat is ful pore for to pay for suche prys þinges
As ȝe haf þryȝt me here þro, suche þre cosses
                         so gode.
              Gawain evades my praise
              As quickly as it is bestowed,
              I can see his guilt weighs
              On him—a very heavy load.

As midnight nears and the knight needs his sleep
He heaps on thanks for our hearth and happy hospitality,
And asking again that as agreed I will assign a man
To trek through the mountains and thickets and thorns
With him to find the flourishing fountain of Flora's faith—
The chapel, the green church, the curse that clouds his
Thoughts—how he ought to have sought it himself, not to
Have taken the trinket that has tainted his troth.
In god fayþe, I say to satisfy him, *wyth a goud wylle*
Al þat euer I yow hyȝt halde schal I redé.

> Indeed
> All I promised will be ready—
> When he enters the chapel of my creed,
> When he fails to hold himself steady,
> When my axe falls to complete the deed.

Once more under the moon Morgan and I undertake our
Rite, raising the Reynarde from the rest I wreaked on him,
And I write on my wife's womb the emblem of our charm—
The five-pointed star that will strike strife into man's heart.
With the last three kisses I confer the magic that makes my child
Swell to full size in Morgan, who holds in her belly the hope
Of all the flora and fauna who fend for themselves against
Man's miserable mistreatment of the meads and meadows,
The rivers and highlands, the mountains and oceans—
Our daughter will dash their dreams with her smoldering
                    red eyes—
          Burning like holly in the snow—
          Like an inferno rising to the skies,
          Like searing embers aglow,
          Like the crimson flames of sunrise.

PASSUS IV

Dawn sparkling with a delightful dusting of frigid diamonds,
The knight kicks off his circuitous quest to my close-by church,
And our company cheerfully frolics out to the courtyard where
My enchantress restores the form of the fowl and fauna, who
Flit and fly and skip and scamper off to their nooks and nests,
Including our ingenious sparrow, who sings her way into the trees.
Morgan draws our star in the sod, and the structure suddenly
Blows away in the breeze, like flakes of snow in a blizzard, leaving
A peaceful prairie of permanent Spring—an oasis for any animal
Wanting warmth in the wild's drawn-out snowy Winters.

                   We leave
          For the green of our glen,
          To give Gawain his reprieve
          And teach a lesson to all men
          Of the vengeance nature can heave.

When we arrive I lie like a star in the lush land of the glen, and
Morgan reforms us—she an enchantress and me an emerald titan.
My bewitching wife restores my strength and strengthens my rigour
So at last I can test the troth of the aristocrat who timidly trots
Toward this sanctified taiga of ancient trees and gentle florets.
Morgan and I enter the blessed boughs of my abbey, where I
Retrieve my cleaver and leave my love until the noble has fled.
He arrives and cries out for the green fiend to deal his blow.
Abyde, I growl, growing again into my green might
And þou schal haf al in hast þat I þe hyȝt ones.

He knows
His lies have sealed his fate
And my axe will bring him low.
And I say to him, *Now, sir swete,*
Of steuen mon may þe trowe.

Gawayn, I greet the gutless guard, *God þe mot loke!*
Iwysse þou art welcom, wyȝe, to my place,
And þou hatz tymed þi trauayl as truee mon schulde,
And þou knowez þe couenauntez kest vus bytwene:
At þis tyme twelmonyth þou toke þat þe falled,
And I schulde at þis Nwe Ȝere ȝeply þe quyte.
And we ar in þis valay verayly oure one;
Here ar no renkes vs to rydde, rele as vus likez.
Haf þy helme of þy hede, and haf here þy pay.
Busk no more debate þen I þe bede þenne
When þou wypped of my hede at a wap one.

         And now
     It's time for him to show
     He has not the bravery of the bough
     That he would chop down in the snow,
     As his flinching will avow.

Raising my razor high in the air I bring it down and he winces.
Þou art not Gawayn, I goad the gent, þat is so goud halden,
Þat neuer arȝed for no here by hylle ne be vale,
And now þou fles for ferde er þou fele harmez!
Such cowardise of þat knyȝt cowþe I neuer here.
Nawþer fyked I ne flaȝe, freke, quen þou myntest,
Ne kest no kauelacion in kyngez hous Arthor.
My hede flaȝ to my fote, and ȝet flaȝ I neuer;
And þou, er any harme hent, arȝez in hert;
Wherfore þe better burne me burde be called
                    þerfore.
         Reddening like a holly berry with shame,
         The knight says he will cower no more,
         But says I cannot lay on him such blame,
         As he cannot pick his head up off the floor.

Haf at þe þenne! I howl, heaving the hatchet high and then
Slicing it swiftly past his stock-still shoulders. I tease him
So, now þou hatz þi hert holle, hitte me bihous.
Halde þe now þe hyȝe hode þat Arþur þe raȝt,
And kepe þy kanel at þis kest, ȝif hit keuer may.
Gawain, enflamed with the same rage that roils through the forest—
The trees long-felt feeling of being helpless as another swings an axe—
Perturbed, petrified, the perjurer impatiently implores me to strike.
For soþe, I cool his temper with terror, *so felly þou spekez,*
I wyl no lenger on lyte lette þin ernde
                    riȝt nowe.
          With this swipe I slice the skin of his neck,
          And for his broken vow, his blood begins to flow.
          He stumbles and starts like a writhing wreck,
          Yelling that by our pact I am only owed one blow.

I laugh *Bolde burne, on þis bent be not so gryndel.*
No mon here vnmanerly þe mysboden habbez,
Ne kyd bot as couenaunde at kyngez kort schaped.
I hyȝt þe a strok and þou hit hatz, halde þe wel payed;
I relece þe of þe remnaunt of ryȝtes alle oþer.
Iif I deliuer had bene, a boffet paraunter
I couþe wroþeloker haf waret, to þe haf wroȝt anger.
Fyrst I mansed þe muryly with a mynt one,
And roue þe wyth no rof-sore, with ryȝt I þe profered
For þe forwarde þat we fest in þe fyrst nyȝt,
And þou trystyly þe trawþe and trwly me haldez,
Al þe gayne þow me gef, as god mon schulde.
Þat oþer munt for þe morne, mon, I þe profered,
Þou kyssedes my clere wyf—þe cossez me raȝtez.
For boþe two here I þe bede bot two bare myntes
                    boute scaþe.
            Trwe mon trwe restore,
            Þenne þar mon drede no waþe.
            At þe þrid þou fayled þore,
            And þerfor þat tappe ta þe.

For hit is my wede þat þou werez, þat ilke wouen girdel,
Myn owen wyf hit þe weued, I wot wel for soþe.
Now know I wel þy cosses, and þy costes als,
And þe wowyng of my wyf: I wroȝt hit myseluen.
I sende hir to asay þe, and sothly me þynkkez
On þe fautlest freke þat euer on fote ȝede;
As perle bi þe quite pese is of prys more,
So is Gawayn, in god fayth, bi oþer gay knyȝtez.
Bot here yow lakked a lyttel, sir, and lewté yow wonted;
Bot þat watz for no wylyde werke, ne wowyng nauþer,
Bot for ȝe lufed your lyf; þe lasse I yow blame.

             Ashamed,
       Gawain curses the belt—
       His pride and troth inflamed,
       A shallow wound so deeply felt,
       A humiliation his scar will proclaim.

I laugh *I halde hit hardily hole, þe harme þat I hade.*
Þou art confessed so clene, beknowen of þy mysses,
And hatz þe penaunce apert of þe poynt of myn egge,
I halde þe polysed of þat plyȝt, and pured as clene
As þou hadez neuer forfeted syþen þou watz fyrst borne;
And I gif þe, sir, þe gurdel þat is golde-hemmed,
For hit is grene as my goune. Sir Gawayn, ȝe maye
Þenk vpon þis ilke þrepe, þer þou forth þryngez
Among prynces of prys, and þis a pure token
Of þe chaunce of þe grene chapel at cheualrous knyȝtez.
And ȝe schal in þis Nwe Ȝer aȝayn to my wonez,
And we schyn reuel þe remnaunt of þis ryche fest
        ful bene.
          Chuckling like a human lord
          I say *With my wyf, I wene,*
          We schal yow wel acorde,
          Þat watz your enmy kene.

Like the seeds of the trees, in this soldier I sow the
Fear that his friends and feats might be false, and I
Shroud my secret scheme when he asks me my name
Þat schal I telle þe trwly, I tell him, lying,
Bertilak de Hautdesert I hat in þis londe.
Þurȝ myȝt of Morgne la Faye, þat in my hous lenges,
And koyntyse of clergye, bi craftes wel lerned,
Þe maystrés of Merlyn mony hatz taken—
For ho hatz dalt drwry ful dere sumtyme
With þat conable klerk, þat knowes alle your knyȝtez
                    at hame;
            Morgne þe goddes
            Þerfore hit is hir name:
            Weldez non so hyȝe hawtesse
            Þat ho ne con make ful tame—

Ho wayned me vpon þis wyse to your wynne halle
For to assay þe surquidré, ȝif hit soth were
Þat rennes of þe grete renoun of þe Rounde Table;
Ho wayned me þis wonder your wyttez to reue,
For to haf greued Gaynour and gart hir to dyȝe
With glopnyng of þat ilke gome þat gostlych speked
With his hede in his honde bifore þe hyȝe table.
Þat is ho þat is at home, þe auncian lady;
Ho is euen þyn aunt, Arþurez half-suster,
Þe duches doȝter of Tyntagelle, þat dere Vter after
Hade Arþur vpon, þat aþel is nowþe.
Þerfore I eþe þe, haþel, to com to þyn aunt,
Make myry in my hous; my meny þe louies,
And I wol þe as wel, wyȝe, bi my faythe,
As any gome vnder God for þy grete trauþe.

                    I lie
            To keep the ground uneven.
            No man may know the reason why
            Flora rose me from my dewy Eden,
            Or that my vengeful child's time is nigh.

I disguise my wife's wisdom and her rightful intent
To best test the timidity and humility of humanity.
Now that they know the woe the wild can wreak—
That their avarice can have an axe at the end of its act—
This should humble their halls and hack at their pride.
They should shy from shearing the riches of the
Fields and the forests, the meads and the meadows,
Should know their knowledge is paltry and partial,
And to balance their boasting and greed with meekness,
For should they not cool the chasms of their cupidity
                    the time
          Of Earth's defender is nigh,
          To demand justice for each crime.
          A scarlet sunset enflames the sky,
          As the chapel bells being to chime.

With Gawain gone, Morgan emerges as the moon magnifies the music,
And dipping the nib of my emerald nail in the thick crimson ink
Of the blood of the embarassed boy I just brought to bow,
I draw the five-pointed star on Morgan that will release our daughter.
In the ages that unfurl our girl grows like the green shoots,
Gentle and graceful, gregarious and good-natured, with the
Might of her mother's magic and the potency of my power.
Her red eyes enlivened with each new lesson of the Earth,
Her emerald face beaming with endearing benevolence.
I teach her to wield the weapon the World awarded her—
                    the flame
          With which to scorch humanity
          Should they forget their shame,
          Or neglect their lesson in humility,
          She will stoke the inferno of blame.

As the sun sets on the Summer of our youth and vigour,
Morgan and I lie down to slumber in the lea where we loved,
Leaving the land in the hands of our formidable child,
To guard the great garden that Flora so sweetly sowed.
And should man's hacking and wrecking wake her
From her sleep in the lava that laps at the bay of Hades,
Once more the magma might be whipped into waves
That will swallow the World in a wash of redress—
The blood that brought her beauty into this world
Demands its duty, or her veins will boil with vengeance.
My blade,
Dulled by the lull of our peaceful life,
No longer needs the blood of the strayed
As our daughter takes up this mission of strife,
So forget not the chapel where I once prayed.

HONY SOYT QUI MAL PENCE

ACKNOWLEDGEMENTS

Thank you to my parents Ruth and Steve Hajnoczky, my sister Julya Hajnoczky, my partner David Tkach, my aunt Carole Roberts, and to all my friends and family for their encouragement.

Thank you to Derek Beaulieu for being an inspiring editor, and to Ian Sampson for the help with the Middle English rhymes.

Thank you to Leigh Nash, Megan Fildes, Julie Wilson, Andrew Faulkner, and to everyone at Invisible who made working on the publication of this book such a wonderful experience.

Bloom & Martyr

Previous versions of some of these poems appeared in the chapbook *Bloom & Martyr*, winner of the 2015 John Lent Poetry Prose Award from Kalamalka Press. Thank you to Jason Dewinetz, kevin mcpherson eckhoff, and everyone at Kalamalka Press for their support and for the beautiful chapbook.

Previous versions of some of these poems also appeared in the publications *Dreamland*, *Lemon Hound*, *New Poetry*, and *Touch the Donkey*. Thank you to Jeremy Stewart, Sina Queyras, George Murray, rob mclennan, and to all those involved with these publications.

Foliage

The following editions of *Sir Gawain and the Green Knight* were consulted during the writing of this poem, listed here in order of frequency of use:

W. S. Merwin, *Sir Gawain & the Green Knight: A New Verse Translation* (New York: Alfred A. Knopf, 2002).

Simon Armitage, *Sir Gawain and the Green Knight* (London: Faber and Faber, 2007).

Sir Gawain and the Green Knight, transcribed from Oxford: Clarendon Press, 1967, Corpus of Middle English Prose and Verse, accessed May 1, 2021, https://quod.lib.umich.edu/c/cme/Gawain.

James Winny, ed. & trans., *Sir Gawain and the Green Knight* (Peterborough, ON: Broadview Press, 1992).

Malcolm Andrew and Ronald Waldron, eds. *The Poems of the Pearl Manuscript: Pearl, Cleanness, Patience, Sir Gawain and the Green Knight, 5th ed.* (Exeter: University of Exeter Press, 2007).

The first stanza of "Foliage" was informed by:

"A Brief History of Geologic Time," *PBS Eons*, 6 November 2017, https://www.youtube.com/watch?v=rWp5ZpJAIAE.

"When Trees Took Over the World," *PBS Eons*, 12 May 2021, https://www.youtube.com/watch?v=UrwMUQbUR30.

INVISIBLE PUBLISHING produces fine Canadian literature for those who enjoy such things. As an independent, not-for-profit publisher, our work includes building communities that sustain and encourage engaging, literary, and current writing.

Invisible Publishing has been in operation for over a decade. We released our first fiction titles in the spring of 2007, and our catalogue has come to include works of graphic fiction and non-fiction, pop culture biographies, experimental poetry, and prose.

We are committed to publishing diverse voices and experiences. In acknowledging historical and systemic barriers, and the limits of our existing catalogue, we strongly encourage writers from LGBTQ2SIA+ communities, Indigenous writers, and writers of colour to submit their work.

Invisible Publishing is also home to the Bibliophonic series of music books and the Throwback series of CanLit reissues.

If you'd like to know more, please get in touch:
info@invisiblepublishing.com

Invisible